Friend Therapy

Celebrating the Blessings of Friendship & Special Times

Inspired by Faith

Friend Therapy
©Product Concept Mfg., Inc.

Friend Therapy
ISBN 978-0-9909508-3-7

Published by Product Concept Mfg., Inc.
2175 N. Academy Circle #200, Colorado Springs, CO 80909

©2015 Product Concept Mfg., Inc. All rights reserved.

Written and Compiled by Linda Staten
in association with Product Concept Mfg., Inc.

Contributions by Patricia Mitchell and Vicki J. Kuyper

All scripture quotations are from the King James version
of the Bible unless otherwise noted.

Scriptures taken from the Holy Bible,
New International Version®, NIV®.
Copyright © 1973, 1978, 1984 by Biblica, Inc.™
Used by permission of Zondervan.
All rights reserved worldwide.
www.zondervan.com

Sayings not having a credit listed are contributed by writers
for Product Concept Mfg., Inc. or in a rare case,
the author is unknown.

Friend Therapy

To Agnes, my forever friend
Love, Nicki

A true friend is the greatest
of all blessings.

La Rochefoucauld

Out of all the people we meet in our lives, only a small number become real friends. Time after time, they're first in line to offer care and support. They have a sixth sense for knowing what we need, whether it's a hug, a helping hand, a gentle (but honest) dose of reality, or the positive power of a cupcake.

Friend Therapy is a little book full of simple, sweet and occasionally silly reminders of the importance of having people we can totally trust and be our true selves with. Anywhere, anytime. It comes with the hope that you will always have individuals in your life who you're lucky to call that very special word, "friend".

A friend is a gift
you give yourself.
Robert Louis Stevenson

Laughter is not at all a bad beginning
for a friendship...
Oscar Wilde

No friendship is an accident.
O. Henry

You Can Call on Me

Laura's car was totally unreliable. But Laura's friend, Kelly, wasn't. So when Laura's car broke down, she called on Kelly.

"So, what's gone out this time?" Kelly asked. "The brakes," Laura replied. "Where are you?" Kelly asked. "The pharmacy," Laura responded. "And where's the car?" Kelly asked. Laura sighed, "In here with me."

I know not whether
our names will be immortal;
I am sure our friendship will.
Walter Savage Landor

This is the day the LORD has made;
we will rejoice and be glad in it.
Psalm 118:24

Setting Sail

Friendship is the only ship
that sails in any weather.
On board there is a crew of two
who travel the years together.
On peaceful days, when all is calm,
the carefree crew can float.
On stormy days, the two stay safe
inside their sturdy boat.
We never know what seas we'll sail.
We can't predict the weather.
Friendship is the only ship
that's built to last forever.

FRIENDS UNDER PRESSURE

Once there were two little lumps
of coal who had been friends for, well,
just about forever. Any time the pressures
of daily life got to be too much, they
shared their feelings and leaned on one
another.

One day a shaft of sunlight broke
through the mine. The two friends could
barely see one another, it was so bright!

"Hey, did you know you're a diamond?" one asked excitedly.

"No, really? Well, guess what! So are you!" the other replied happily.

The two friends hurried out into the sunlight together, and they're still sparkling to this very day.

No one friend can offer everything,
but every friend offers something
that no one else can.

Friendship is a strong
and habitual inclination in two persons
to promote the good and happiness
of one another.
Eustace Budgell

Friendship is equality.
Pythagoras

Loyalty is what we seek
in friendship.
Cicero

LET ME TELL YOU ABOUT MY FRIEND

My friend cares how I really feel.
My quirks and moods are no big deal.
She's there to help me keep it real
when things get out of whack.
She'll tell me when I need a mint
or I'm wearing too much leopard print.
When I'm confused, she'll drop a hint.
She's always got my back.

My friend won't skimp on compliments.
She's "all ears" when I need to vent.
She's on my side, a thousand percent,
whether we're near or far.
She truly knows what I'm all about.
She's part of me, and there's no doubt,
she's someone I couldn't do without.
My friend – that's what you are.

The Family Tree of Friendship

Friends come in all shapes and sizes, ages and bloodlines. Sometimes, the roots of friendship begin at birth. Mothers, sisters, daughters...we're often blessed by being born, or adopted, into a family of lifelong friends.

Other friends begin as strangers. A chance meeting, a mutual acquaintance, a shared interest or casual conversation can all herald a new addition to our chosen family—the circle of friends that complete our lives by filling our hearts with joy.

Whether related by blood or experience, it's in the company of these amazing women that we have the privilege to grow and grieve, live and learn, laugh and love.

To be happy,
the wise heart recommends:
Treat your friends like family
and your family like friends!

How many things,
which for our own sake we should never do,
do we perform for the sake of our friends.
Cicero

It isn't so much what's on
the table that matters,
as what's on the chairs.
W. S. Gilbert

Is there anything quite as comforting
or comfortable as good friends
gathered around the kitchen table?

FRIENDSHIP – WHAT A TREAT!

An office party was planned to welcome Sara, a new employee who had just moved to the city. Michelle decided that for once, instead of store bought, she would bring a batch of home-baked cookies.

Michelle never, ever baked, but she remembered a simple recipe she'd seen recently in some magazine or other. It sounded so easy, even she could do it.

Michelle bought the ingredients and got started. Honey, carrots, peanut butter, oatmeal, and flour. The kitchen smelled so unusual that her dog Louie came in to check it out.

The next morning Michelle noticed that overnight, her cookies had turned rock hard. It was too late to run to the store, though.

As everyone assembled, Michelle stared at the impressive array of goodies.

The next morning, Michelle saw Sara heading toward her desk with the container in her hands. It was empty.

"Hi. I just wanted to return this and say thanks so much for the wonderful treats." Sara had a big smile on her face. "You're the one who baked these, right?"

"Well, unfortunately, yes," Michelle blushed slightly.

"Benny loved them! He ate every single one!" Renee laughed.

"Really? They were so hard," Michelle replied. She couldn't imagine a kid eating one of her baking mistakes, let alone all of them.

"Oh, no, they were just right. And chewing them stimulated Benny's gums, too," Sara said enthusiastically.

"Huh?" Michelle was getting confused. "Well, that's, um, good. I guess."

"Anyway, everyone **was** really nice to welcome me yesterday," Sara said, "but you're the only person who was so thoughtful, you even brought something to welcome my dog."

Suddenly Michelle recalled where she had seen the recipe. It **was** in a magazine at the veterinarian's clinic.

"Hey, do you know of a good dog park?" Sara asked.

"As a matter of fact, I **do**," Michelle responded brightly.

And that was the start of one beautiful friendship. Well, actually, **two**.

WOMEN WORTH HANGING OUT WITH...

- assure you that you have an hourglass figure, even when the sands of time begin to shift.

- don't bat an eye when you order a side of chocolate chips with your salad.

- may witness you making a fool of yourself, yet don't believe it's a permanent condition.

A friend is one who knows you as you are,
understands where you've been,
accepts who you've become,
and still gently invites you to grow.

GRATED EXPECTATIONS

Once there were two lemons who were fabulous friends. They "got" one another. They gave each other the giggles. They had adventures. It's just how they rolled.

One day, one of the lemons asked, "Should we make lemonade?"
"Huh?" the other replied.

"Well, you know, everyone always says that when you have lemons, you're supposed to make lemonade."

"You're right. It's tradition," the other agreed. "And you and I always do what's expected of us."

The two friends gazed at one another for a moment. Then they burst out laughing, and went off to make the world's most decadent lemon meringue pie. (Heavy on the meringue!) It's just how they rolled.

Good fences make good neighbors.
That's what the poets state.
But if you want to make good friends,
be sure to add a gate.

Open House

We just shake hands at meeting
With many that come nigh;
We nod the head in greeting
To many that go by.
But welcome through the gateway
Our few old friends and true;
Then hearts leap up and straightway
There's open house for you,
Old friends,
there's open house for you!

Gerald Massey

Keeping It All in the Family

A daughter goes to visit her aging mother in the senior living center.

As she's waiting for her mother to wake up from her afternoon nap, she notices a bowl of peanuts beside her mother's bed and helps herself to one.

As time passes, and her mother continues to sleep, the daughter polishes off the entire bowl.

When her mother wakes up the daughter says apologetically, "Mom! I'm so sorry, but it looks like I finished off all your peanuts."

"That's okay, honey," her Mom replies. "Without my teeth, all I can do is suck the chocolate off and then spit them back in the bowl anyway."

TIME TOGETHER

We're like two clocks keeping time, side-by-side. We know what makes each other tick—and, wow, can we "talk." We can unwind, charge each other's batteries or even sound an alarm in the other's presence, all while feeling perfectly comfortable displaying our true face.

We make time for one another, regardless of how crazy our schedules may be. And every hour, minute or second we share in each other's company is always time well spent.

The true test of friendship is to be able
to sit or walk with a friend for an hour in
perfect silence without wearying of
one another's company.
Dinah Maria Mulock Craik

Once in an age,
God sends to some of us
a friend who loves in us...
not the person we are,
but the angel we may be.
Harriet Beecher Stowe

Angels On Call

Those we love are angels in disguise.

They ring us up for no reason— just to say, "Halo."

If we need help anytime, anywhere, they're always ready to wing it.

Their smile never fails to lift our spirits and provide us with a bit of heaven here on earth.

Call it a blessing.
Call it a gift.
Call it an answered prayer.
Call it a touch
of heaven on earth—
the bond that old friends share.

It is my joy in life to find
At every turning of the road
The strong arm of a comrade kind
To help me onward with my load;
And since I have no gold to give,
And love alone must make amends,
My only prayer is, while I live—
God make me worthy of my friends.
F. D. Sherman

The only way to have a friend is to be one.
Ralph Waldo Emerson

THE HIKE

Generally, Grace and Jen tended to avoid exercise at all costs. They much preferred book clubs, concerts and board games.

Nevertheless, they decided to give it a try. Jen suggested they take a long hike, so they headed off for the nature preserve.

"I don't think we can do it," Grace said as she inspected a map of all the trails.

"We'll be fine," Jen confidently replied.

"But let's face it. We're both out of shape," Grace reminded her friend. "How do you think we're going to manage this?"

"Piece of cake!" Jen said. "We'll only hike on trails that go downhill."

Good Friends Don't Count

...how many trips you make to
the buffet table.

...the birthday candles on your cake.

...the number of times you've lost the
same five pounds.

...the favors they do for you.

...the mistakes you've made.

A friend is a gift you give yourself.
Robert Louis Stevenson

Friendship is like money,
easier made than kept.
Samuel Butler

A friend loveth at all times.
Proverbs 17:17

You Could Use a Friend When...

Linda absent-mindedly grabbed her husband's glasses, instead of her own, as she hurriedly left for work one morning. Though the prescription was close, it was not close enough. Linda was only a few minutes from home when she was pulled over by a state trooper.

"Ma'am, is there a reason why you were weaving all over the road?" he asked.

"Officer, thank goodness you're here!" Linda said, visibly relieved. "I almost had an accident! I looked up and there was a tree right in front of me! I swerved to the left and there was another tree right in front of me. Then I swerved right and there was STILL a tree right in front of me!"

"Ma'am," the officer responded, gesturing towards the rearview mirror, "that's your air freshener."

Lots of people know "stuff",
but it takes a real friend to know *you*.

Friendship requires great communication.
Francis de Sales

Two dear old friends
strolled side by side.
They didn't speak a word.
But in their minds,
they talked and talked,
and in their hearts,
they heard.

PENNIES FROM HEAVEN

One day, while Lena and Carol were out together, Lena found a penny on the sidewalk. She stooped to pick it up, held it to the light and smiled.

"Why on earth are you smiling? It's just a penny," Carol laughed.

"Because it was made the year I was born," Lena replied. "When I was little, my grandma told me that every time I found a penny from the year I was born, it was a penny from heaven, reminding me to be happy because I was put on earth that year for a special reason." And with that, Lena tucked the penny in her pocket.

It wasn't too very long after that that Lena's life turned into one long string of difficulties. Sometimes it all felt overwhelming to Lena, but Carol was always there to lean on. And every time the two friends went out, Lena found a penny somewhere or other with her birth year on it. It never failed to lift her spirits, and Carol always looked just as tickled as Lena when it happened.

One evening during dinner at their favorite cafe, Carol handed Lena her purse to hold while she went to the restroom. As Lena waited, someone bumped her arm, and Carol's purse tipped over, spilling its contents onto the table.

As Lena began to put everything back into the handbag, she noticed a clear plastic coin purse full of nothing but pennies. Out of curiosity, she held it up and squinted at the coins. Her eyes widened. Every single penny was stamped with the year Lena was born. Just as Lena placed the last of the items into the handbag, Carol returned to the table.

They strolled out the front door toward the parking lot.

"Why the big smile?" Carol asked. "Find a penny from heaven?"

"Why, yes," Lena said as she gave her friend a hug, "I certainly did."

What joy is better than news of friends?
Robert Browning

Which of all my important nothings
shall I tell you first?
Jane Austen

My friends are my estate.
Emily Dickinson

Small service is true service while it lasts.
Of humblest friends,
bright creature! scorn not one:
The daisy, by the shadow that it casts,
Protects the lingering dew-drop
from the sun.
William Wordsworth

In friendship
we find nothing false or insincere;
everything is straightforward,
and springs from the heart.
Cicero

The truth is the kindest thing we can
give folks in the end.
Harriet Beecher Stowe

The supreme happiness of life
is the conviction of being loved for yourself,
or, more correctly,
being loved in spite of yourself.
Victor Hugo

Life Luggage

We all have emotional baggage. Maybe it's one little case. Maybe it's a whole matching set accumulated over decades of simply being ourselves! But no matter what kind of emotional baggage we've got, it can get heavy. Having a little help with it now and then makes all the difference. That's where friends come in.

They add their strength to our strength and together, we share the weight. Friends are like those little wheels on the bottom that let us run to where we need to be in our journeys through life, pulling all our inner "stuff" behind us.

But friends don't just help us carry our loads. They know what we've got inside all that emotional baggage, and they love us enough to tell us when we've packed too much.

They're the ones we can depend upon to say, "Do you really need all those re-grets?" or "If you get rid of that guilt, you'll have room for self-confidence!"

Why do friends do all that? Because they care. Because they know we will do the same for them. And maybe, just maybe, because they realize that as we journey through life, we'll find some really great souvenirs along the way. Friends – they're the people who remind us to leave room for the good stuff, too.

TRUE CONFESSIONS

"My husband tried to cook while I was away on my business trip," Jean told her friend over lunch at their favorite restaurant.

"So, how did it go?" Tami asked.

"Not so well," Jean confided. "He said every recipe he tried was so demanding, he never got past the first line."

"What do you mean?" said Tami.

"They all started with, 'Take a clean dish...'"

A FRIENDLY REQUEST

Pam wanted her good friend, Jean, to enroll with her in a yoga class.

"Absolutely not!" Jean exclaimed. "I tried that once!"

"What happened?" Pam asked.

"I twisted, hopped, jumped, stretched and pulled," Jean replied. "And by the time I got my yoga pants on the class was over!"

Friendship make prosperity
more shining and lessens adversity
by dividing and sharing it.
Cicero

Use what talents you possess.
The woods would be very silent
if no birds sang there
except those that sang best.
Henry Van Dyke

THE VOICE OF A FRIEND

Abby's best friend Ming loved to sing. Every time Ming heard there was karaoke somewhere, she'd grab Abby and they'd go. Ming sang karaoke at the mall, the community theater, even church socials. And every time she did, Abby would clap like crazy.

One day while Ming was on stage at a street fair, a man standing next to Abby leaned over and whispered, "Your friend has quite a unique voice. I've never heard singing quite like it." The man smiled.

"Oh, yeah. Ming's totally tone deaf," Abby laughed, "but singing really makes her happy." Ming's song ended at that moment and Abby applauded loudly.

No one else in the crowd knew what Abby knew—that when you really needed advice, a word of encouragement or the right thing said at just the right time, there was no voice quite like Ming's. It was perfect.

THE SECRET

"Oh, my gosh. Were you sick? And you didn't tell me?" Marie exclaimed as she walked into Jan's living room. Several get well cards were prominently displayed over the fireplace.

"Uh, no big deal. Let's go do something fun," Jan suggested.

"Are you sure you're up to it?" Marie asked. She walked over to the mantle.

"Definitely, and time's a-wasting," Jan said brightly, as she quickly began to gather up the cards.

Marie grabbed an oversized, cartoony card that looked oddly familiar, and peeked inside. There was a message in her handwriting. She had sent the card several years ago when her good friend broke her arm. She looked at Jan in surprise.

"Okay, okay, I confess!" Jan threw up her hands. "I wasn't sick. I keep those cards for an emergency."

"What kind of emergency?" Marie asked.

"My whole family was coming over, and I wanted them to think I was too sick to clean the house."

Thus nature has
no love for solitude
and always leans,
as it were,
on some support;
and the sweetest
support is found
in the most
intimate friendship.
Cicero

Life is a beautiful question
to which friendship is
often the answer.

There is nothing I would not do
for those who are really my friends.
I have no notion of loving people by halves,
it is not my nature.
Jane Austen

THE FEAST

There's an ancient tale about a woman who had had a very hard life. One evening at bedtime she prayed that an angel would visit her and remind her of what happiness is.

That very night, the angel came to the woman in a dream. She took her to a great hall. Inside there was a long wooden table filled with golden plates and cups. Each plate was full of wonderful food, and each cup had something refreshing to drink. Every person who sat at the table had stiff casts on both arms, which made it impossible for the guests to put any of the food or drink to their lips. They were strangers, so they sat and sat, staring at their full plates, hungry and silent. The angel said to the woman, "This is unhappiness."

Then the angel led the woman to another great hall. Inside there was a long wooden table, just like the first, filled with more golden plates and cups. People sat in all the chairs, and every guest had stiff casts on both arms. Their plates and cups were empty, but they were talking and laughing with one another.

"Why are they smiling when their plates are empty?" the woman asked the angel.

"They are friends. Though their circumstances kept them from feeding themselves, they could reach out and feed one another," the angel replied. "And this is happiness."

Ay, there are some good things in life,
That fall not away with the rest.
And, of all best things upon earth,
I hold that a faithful friend is the best.
Owen Meredith

To have a best friend
is to have a second heart.

Best friend, my well-spring in the wilderness!
George Eliot

WHERE'S THE BEEF?

"Inflation is getting out of hand!" Margo complained to her best friend.

"Yesterday I went to a fancy restaurant and ordered a forty dollar steak. I told the waiter to put it on my credit card— and it fit!"

Laugh and the world laughs with you.
Cry and your friend might be
forced to dig out that used fast food napkin
at the bottom of her purse.

THE TURTLE AND THE RABBIT

A turtle and a rabbit both loved to run. One day they met at a race being held in the forest. As they wished each other good luck, the buzzer sounded and they were off. Competitors kept dropping out until finally, the turtle and the rabbit were the only two runners left.

The turtle arrived first at a wide stream and started swimming. She heard the rabbit on shore.

"I can't do this. I'm afraid of water!" the rabbit shouted. "I give up!"

The turtle turned around and swam back to shore.

"Here. Hop on my back!" the turtle said, and they crossed the stream, the rabbit holding on with her eyes tightly shut.

On the other shore they resumed racing. They came to a huge log blocking the path. The rabbit hopped over and kept running. Then she heard the turtle behind her.

"Oh, no!" the turtle cried. She had fallen on her back. "I'm stuck. I give up."

The rabbit hopped back to the log.

"Grab my tail and hold on," the rabbit shouted.

The turtle held on tightly, even though the rabbit's fuzzy tail was tickling her nose. When they got over the log, the rabbit landed gently.

They were almost at the finish line when the turtle and the rabbit winked at one another and stopped in their tracks.

The stunned crowd looked on in silence. The head judge cleared his throat.

"Excuse me, ladies, but this is a competition," he said with great authority. "There can only be one winner."

"Oh, never mind that!" the turtle exclaimed. "We're both winners!"

"If we hadn't helped one another, neither of us would have gotten this far!" the rabbit added.

And the turtle and the rabbit strolled off into the forest to a really cute café with great lettuce and veggies.

Moral: Wherever you're going in life, it helps to have friends to hold onto.

Friends Are Like Coffee

You're smooth under pressure
And strong if I need it.
Any expectation?
You're sure to exceed it.
You make me feel confident,
Joyful and whole.
Yes, a good friend is like
Caffeine for my soul!

Vicki J. Kuyper

No one is useless in this world
who lightens the burdens of another.
Charles Dickens

It is not so much our friends' help that
helps us as the confident knowledge
that they will help us.
Epicurus

Do good to thy friend to keep him.
Benjamin Franklin

Two people are better than one,
because they have a good return
for their labour.
Ecclesiastes 4:9

PUTTING THE PIECES TOGETHER

Edna was Lucille's best friend at the retirement center. So when Edna asked for help with a jigsaw puzzle, Lucille immediately sat down, ready to get to work.

Edna explained, "It's a really tough puzzle and I can't even figure out how to start."

"Well, Edna," said Lucille patiently, "what's the picture supposed to look like when you're finished?"

"A rooster," Edna said.

Lucille took a look at the box and then the puzzle pieces. Then she gently put her hand on her friend's shoulder.

"Relax, Edna," Lucille said. "I'll go get us each a nice cup of tea. Then I'll help you put all the corn flakes back in the box."

My friend is one…
who takes me for what I am.
Henry David Thoreau

Never forget
the days I spent with you.
Continue to be my friend,
as you will always
find me yours.
Ludwig van Beethoven

You and your circle of friends know you're getting older when

    ... the gleam in your eye is from the sun hitting your bifocals.

    ... you accidentally enter your password on the microwave.

    ... you wake up looking like your driver's license photo.

    ... you try to straighten out the wrinkles in your socks and discover you aren't wearing any.

As gold more splendid
from the fire appears,
Thus friendship brightens
by the length of years.
Thomas Carlyle

Everyone must have felt that a cheerful
friend is like a sunny day,
which sheds its brightness on all around.
John Lubbock

The very society of joy redoubles it;
so that, while it lights upon my friend
it rebounds upon myself,
and the brighter his candle burns,
the more easily will it light mine.
Robert South

THE TWO LITTLE CANDLES

Once there was a little candle that couldn't hold a flame no matter how hard it tried. Seemed as if there was always a breeze here or a raindrop there.

One day it met another little candle who had a beautiful flame.

"Pardon me for saying it, but you've really got a glow," the plain little candle said.

"Thanks, but I bet you can really shine, too," the bright little candle replied.

"Well, I try," the candle replied. "but life just keeps happening."

"I know just what you mean. Hey, I've got an idea. Lean on me," the bright little candle said. And as the plain candle leaned, there was a spark, and the bright candle's flame passed to the other. Now both little candles were casting a warm, lovely light everywhere.

From that time on, they were such good friends. Nothing made them happier than when they were both shining brightly. Any time a gust of wind or a splash of rain put out one candle's flame, they huddled close and one would relight the other, without even being asked.

Moral: A friend not only sees you in your best light—she helps you find it.

We cannot tell the precise moment
when friendship is formed.
As in filling a vessel drop by drop,
there is at last a drop
which makes it run over;
so in a series of kindnesses
there is at last one
which makes the heart run over.
James Boswell

A kind heart is a fountain of gladness,
making everything in its vicinity
freshen into smiles.
Washington Irving

Without wearing any mask
we are conscious of,
we have a special face for each friend.
Oliver Wendell Holmes

Friendship Time Line

At 15 you and your friends decide to eat at the burger joint next to the "nice restaurant" because you only have $4.53 combined between the four of you—and that cute boy in history class works there.

At 25, your same group of friends meets at the "nice restaurant," because it has free appetizers and stays open late.

At 35, you meet there because it's close to the gym.

45...because they have low-fat options on the menu.

At 55...because the lighting is bright enough to read the menu.

At 65...because they have an early bird special.

At 75...because it's handicap accessible and the food isn't too spicy.

At 85...because you want to try something new...and none of you can remember having eaten there before.

Give what you have.
To someone it may be better
than you dare to think.
Henry Wadsworth Longfellow

Behold, I do not give lectures
or a little charity,
When I give, I give myself.
Walt Whitman

Just being in your company
makes me believe I'm on vacation.
You turn even the smallest joy
into full-blown celebration.
You act as though loving others well
is your personal vocation.
That's why you're more than just a friend—
You're my inspiration!
Vicki J. Kuyper

The real voyage of discovery
consists not in seeking new landscapes
but in having new eyes.
Marcel Proust

A friend helps you see the bright side of life,
even if you both have to squint.

The best thing we can find in our travels
is an honest friend.
He is a fortunate voyager who finds many.
Robert Louis Stevenson

It is a friendly heart that has plenty of friends.
William Makepeace Thackeray

The blessing of true friendship
shines a light
on all the other blessings
in our lives.

The true atmosphere of friendship
is a sunny one.
Griefs and disappointments do not thrive
in its clear, healthy light.
Randolph Bourne

A true friend sees the
goodness in you,
and reflects back to you
the very best of who you are.

My Friends Rock

Before I lay me down to sleep,
I pray, dear Lord, my friends you'll keep
Happy, healthy and full of laughter,
From this day forward until long after
Our hair turns gray or white or blue
And every day all that we do
Is sit around and reminisce
About good times, good friends... such bliss!
'Cuz though we can't turn back the clock
My friends and I will always ROCK!

Vicki J. Kuyper

There is nothing more
special than a good friend—
Except a good friend who grows
to be an old friend.

REALITY CHECK

"So, how did your annual physical go?"
Sarah asked her friend, Susan.

"Horrible!" Susan said. "The nurse
asked how much I weighed and I said,
'135.' Then she put me on the scale and
it said I weighed 180!

Then the nurse asked for my height. I
said, 'Five feet four inches.' She said, 'I only
measure 5' 2".'

Next she took my blood pressure and
said it was really high. That's when I lost it!"

"What did you do?" Sarah asked.

"I screamed, 'Of course it's high! When
I came in here I was like a fairy princess,
tall and slender—now you're telling me I'm
one of the seven dwarves!'"

Friendship is never established
as an understood relation.
It is a miracle
which requires constant proofs.
It is an exercise of the purest imagination
and of the rarest faith...
The language of Friendship
is not words, but meanings.
It is an intelligence above language.
Henry David Thoreau

Treat your friends
as you do your pictures,
and place them in their best light.
Jennie Jerome Churchill

A friend may well be reckoned
the masterpiece of nature.
Ralph Waldo Emerson

Blest be the tie that binds
Our hearts in Christian love;
The fellowship of kindred minds
Is like to that above.
John Fawcett

Oh, the comfort—
The inexpressible comfort of
feeling safe with a person—
Having neither to weigh thoughts,
Nor measure words, but pouring them
All right out just as they are—
Chaff and grain together;
Certain that a faithful hand
will take and sift them,
keep what is worth keeping,
and then with the breath of kindness
blow the rest away.
Dinah Maria Mulock Craik

Make new friends but keep the old.
They know the secrets
that you don't want told!
(Tee-hee!)

Wishing to be friends
is quick work,
but friendship is a slow-ripening fruit.
Aristotle

To have a good friend
is one of the highest
delights of life;
to be a good friend is
one of the noblest
and most difficult
undertakings.

Anonymous

WANTED: ONE TERRIFIC FRIEND

We all have unwritten job descriptions for our friends. Not only do we expect them to be fun to hang out with, we often rely on them to be our most candid sounding boards.

At any given moment, we expect them to fill the role of mentor, teacher, mother, sister, stylist, financial planner, coach, therapist or cheerleader.

In the midst of all those expectations, let's not forget to also expect them to be human. We all fail from time to time—us, and our friends. Let's extend to each other the grace to fail, as well as fly. That's what true love, and friendship, is all about.

THE LIFE LESSON

Having been laid off from her teaching position several months earlier, Sophia was certain she'd have no trouble finding a new job. She had experience, great references, a solid education and a willingness to move anywhere—even far away from her wonderful circle of friends.

Sophia carefully crafted a cover letter and attached a copy of her current résumé. Then she emailed it to over two-dozen prospective employers.

A week went by. Then two. There was no response to her email. Sophia began to get anxious about not having received a single request for an interview. Perhaps finding a job was going to be much more difficult than she'd first believed.

Finally, one morning she saw a reply in her email in-box. Anxiously, she clicked to open it. The email read:

Dear Ms. Greene, Your résumé was not attached as stated. However, I would like to thank you for the wonderful Fettuccine Alfredo recipe.

Sincerely, Janet Pierce
Principal, Perkins Middle School

Madame de Staël is such a good friend,
she would throw all her aquaintances
in the water for the pleasure of fishing
them out again.
Charles Maurice de Talleyrand

Friendship is a word the very sight of which
in print makes the heart warm.
Augustine Birrell

I want a warm and faithful friend
To cheer the adverse hour;
Who ne'er to flatter will descend,
Nor bend the knee to power,—
A friend to chide me when I'm wrong,
My inmost soul to see;
And that my friendship prove as strong
For him as his for me.

John Quincy Adams

Friend Therapy

All friends are different,
unique and quite rare,
but with one thing in common –
they totally care!
Whether you've known them
for weeks or for years,
good friends share everything,
smiles and tears.
Are those silver linings
a bit in doubt?
A friend stands by you
and points them out.
Would it help to relax,
to forget and have fun?
A friend knows what's needed
to get the job done!

Are you feeling confused?
A bit tired or hurt?
Friends prescribe hugs
(oh, and sometimes dessert!)
Friends are 24/7.
You just text or call
to go cry on the couch
or go laugh at the mall.
It's true about friends,
though it's pretty cliche –
they know you,
but still love you anyway!
Ask any woman
and she will agree
that nothing compares
to friend therapy!

It is great to have friends when one is young, but indeed it is still more so when you are getting old.

When we are young,
friends are like everything else,
a matter of course. In the old days,
we know what it means to have them.
Edvard Grieg

They were two old friends,
the boomer kind.
Life could be hard
but they didn't mind.
They knew all the words
and they'd sing along
when the radio played
golden oldie songs.
Though they joked
that their brains were getting slow,
they'd forgotten more
than most folks know.
And they grooved through the decades
without a care,
like they still had flowers
in their hair.

We have been friends together
in sunshine and in shade.
Caroline Norton

Friendship is a sheltering tree.
Samuel Taylor Coleridge

A friend can see
what's invisible to the eye
because she looks with the heart.

A little word in kindness spoken,
A motion or a tear,
Has often healed the heart that's broken,
And made a friend sincere.
Daniel Clement Colesworthy

What sunshine is to flowers,
smiles are to humanity.
They are but trifles to be sure;
but, scattered along life's pathway,
the good they do is inconceivable.
Joseph Addison

A kind word
is God's love
in the voice
of a friend.

Two persons cannot long be friends
if they cannot forgive each other's
little failings.
Jean de la Bruyere

Friends see what's invisible
to the eye because they
look with the heart.

MISTAKEN IDENTITY

Once every year, three well-to-do sisters got together to catch up on their lives—and talk about what they'd sent their hard-to-please mother for her birthday.

"This year, I sent Mom a Mercedes AND a driver," the first said proudly.

The second said, "I can top that! I built her a new house!"

The eldest daughter said, with a confident smile, "I've got you both beat. You know how Mom enjoys reading Shakespeare, but can't see very well? I sent her a parrot that can recite the entire works of Shakespeare. It took hundreds of grad students over twelve years to teach him. I had to pledge $20,000 a year for 20 years to the university's theater program to compensate them for their beloved mascot. But it's worth it!"

Soon after, the daughters received their thank you notes.

To the first daughter, the mother wrote, "I'm too old to travel. I stay home all the time, so I never use the car—and the driver is rude."

To the second daughter she wrote, "The house is too big. I live in only one room and still have to clean all the rest."

To the eldest daughter she wrote, "Dearest, you're the only daughter to have the good sense to know what your mother likes. The chicken was delicious."

My treasures are my friends.
Constantius

Always run errands
with your best friend.
She'll insist on going
to the tiara store first.

GROCERY STORE GIGGLES

Lauren was in the supermarket bright and early. As she pushed her cart down the cookie aisle, she saw a little girl begging her mother for cookies. When the girl's mother said, "No" the little girl began screaming at the top of her lungs.

In a quiet voice, the mother kept repeating, "Don't get excited, Monica. Don't scream, Monica. Don't be upset, Monica. Don't yell, Monica. Keep calm, Monica."

At the check-out counter Lauren wound up behind the young mother. She commented, "I couldn't help noticing how patient you were with little Monica!"

The woman replied, "I'm Monica!"

If instead of a gem, or even a flower,
we should cast the gift of a loving thought
into the heart of a friend,
that would be giving as the angels give.
George McDonald

I can't imagine this journey without
someone like you by my side.
You're like the chocolate chips
in the trail mix of my life.

To get the full value of joy,
you must have somebody to divide it with.
Mark Twain

The expensiveness of friendship does not
lie in what one does for one's friends,
but in what, out of regard for them,
one leaves undone.
Henrik Ibsen

If we would build on a sure foundation
in friendship, we must love our friends
for their sakes rather than for our own;
we must look at their truth to themselves
full as much as their truth to us.

Charlotte Bronte

One friend said to another,
"My daughter seems to be getting
a lot out of her college courses.
She's very bright, you know.
Every time we get an email from her,
we have to take out the dictionary."
Her friend replied, "You're so lucky!
Every time we hear from our daughter
we have to take out a loan!"

Two may talk together
under the same roof for many years,
yet never really meet;
and two others at first speech
are old friends.
Mary Catherwood

When the heart overflows with gratitude
or with any other sweet and
sacred sentiment,
what is the word to which it would
give utterance?
A friend.
Walter Savage Landor

Father of all mankind,
make the roof of my house wide
enough for all opinions,
oil the door of my house so it opens easily
to friend and stranger, and set such a table
in my house that my whole family may speak
kindly and freely around it.
Hawaiian Prayer

Blessed is the influence of one true,
loving human soul on another.
George Eliot

Encourage one another
and build each other up,
just as in fact you are doing.
I Thessalonians 5:11 NIV

HEAVENLY HOME RUN

Celia was devastated when she found out her best friend, Dorothy, was ill. Celia visited Dorothy in the hospital every day, where they laughed and relived memories from the years they'd shared together.

They reminisced about their winning seasons on the women's softball league in high school, then in college and later on with their church league. Celia jokingly told Dorothy that if there was a women's softball team in heaven she'd have something to look forward to. Later that night, Dorothy died.

Celia was awakened shortly afterward by a flash of light. She heard Dorothy's voice calling to her out of the darkness, "Celia!" she heard her friend whisper, "I have good news and I have bad news!"

"Go ahead, Dorothy," Celia replied. "I can take it."

Dorothy's voice continued, "The good news is there IS a team! The bad news is you're pitching on Tuesday."

A Circle of Friends

Have you ever wondered why we always call our relationship with our friends a circle? Why not a square, a triangle, or a star? There are plenty of other shapes we could use to symbolize the special bond we share with our friends, but somehow a circle just seems right.

Maybe it's because a circle has no sharp edges. Nothing that could cut or hurt us. Maybe it's because there are no corners in which to hide or feel trapped. Everything is right there, open and honest. Perhaps a circle is the right symbol because everyone is equal in a circle. No one is bigger or has more importance. Everyone is equally close to the heart of it all.

Who knows? It might even be because a circle can roll like a wheel. It can move and go places. And when it rolls, friends take turns giving support to the rest of the circle. And unlike other shapes, a circle can become larger or smaller and still remain perfectly round and encompassing.

Whatever the reason, a circle of friends is a wonderful thing to be part of. May yours always be unbroken.

Always I have a chair for you in the smallest
parlor in the world, to wit, my heart.
Emily Dickinson

We are advertised by our loving friends.
William Shakespeare

ROAD TRIP

Three friends were driving down the highway at a very slow speed. A patrolman pulled them over and said that driving so slowly could be hazardous for other drivers.

The driver explained that she was following the posted limit: 20 miles per hour.

"Ma'am," the officer said, trying to hide a smile, "that sign indicates you are traveling on Highway 20."

"Well," the woman replied, "that explains why Lisa has been so quiet back there. Apparently we just turned off of Highway 125."

Some people say impulse shopping,
eating too much chocolate and letting the
housework go is a symptom of aging,
depression and stress.
I call it "a perfect day with friends."

I know my friend.
Feel free to ask me
anything about her.
The only thing
I wouldn't know
is what I'd do without her!

THE GIFT

"Well, what happened?" Amy asked Mags over the phone. They lived some distance away but stayed in touch.

"Ah, you mean the birthday gift," Mags replied.

"Yes. I'm dying of curiosity!" Amy said excitedly.

"Well, you know what I was wishing for," Mags said.

"And dropping big hints for," Amy teased.

"Yep. My dream machine. Something shiny that goes from zero to 150 in a couple of seconds when you put your foot down. That's what I told him," Mags said.

"Soooo…did your husband get the hints?"

"Amy, I wish you were here to see it for yourself. I'm still stunned!"

"Oh my gosh, I can't stand it. Send me a photo right now!"

They hung up and few minutes later, Amy's cellphone dinged. She opened up Mags' text message, and stared in disbelief at the photo. There it was, with a big bow still on it. The gift. A brand new bathroom scale.

A TRUE FRIEND is someone who

    … remembers your birthday,
       but forgets your age.

    … says nice things about you behind
       your back.

    … will take *your* call, even if she's told
       her secretary she's unavailable.

    … only keeps a secret from you when
       she's planning your surprise party.

    … knows everything about you, but
       loves you anyway.

FAIR GAME

You know you and the women you love
are getting older when you come home
from the county fair feeling sore all over—
and all you've ridden is the massage chair.

The belief that youth is the happiest time of
life is founded on a fallacy.
The happiest person is the person who
thinks the most interesting thoughts,
and we grow happier as we grow older.
William Lyon Phelps

Let your boat of life be light,
packed only with what you need—
a homely home and simple pleasures,
one or two friends worth the name,
someone to love
and someone to love you.
Jerome K. Jerome

I count myself in nothing else so happy,
As in a soul rememb'ring my good friends.
William Shakespeare

Perhaps the most delightful friendships
are those in which there is much agreement,
much disputation,
and yet more personal liking.
George Eliot

Games to Play With Our
Friends as We Age

- Sag, You're It
- Hide and Go To Sleep
- Pin the Toupe on the Bald Guy
- Musical Recliners
- Simon Says...Something Incoherent

FRIENDS SHARE EVERYTHING

Two elderly women who'd been friends for more than 70 years walked slowly into a fast food restaurant and ordered a single kids' meal. Settling themselves into a booth, they carefully cut the solitary burger in half and divided the small bag of fries, one-by-one, between them. Next, they took turns taking one sip of soda from the cup. Finally, one lady began slowly eating her half of the burger, while the other sat patiently, waiting her turn to eat.

Surmising the elderly women didn't have enough money to purchase meals of their own (and secretly hoping that when she grew older she'd enjoy as sweet a friendship as these two women seemed to share) a young woman offered to order them another meal.

The woman who was eating smiled and said, "Thank you, but we're fine." She continued chewing her half of the burger while her friend continued watching. Again, the young women felt compelled to offer her assistance. But once again, the elderly woman reassured her that they were just fine. They enjoyed sharing everything.

The young woman turned to the woman who hadn't started her meal yet and asked, "If you enjoy sharing everything so much, what are you waiting for?"

"The teeth," the woman replied.

The best mirror is an old friend.
George Herbert

There is no friend like an old friend
who has shared our morning days,
no greeting like his welcome,
no homage like his praise.
Oliver Wendell Holmes, Sr.

We are all travellers
in the wilderness of this world,
and the best we can find in our
travels is an honest friend.
Robert Louis Stevenson

The key is to keep company
only with people who uplift you,
whose presence calls forth your best.
Epictetus

May God grant you
and the friends you love...
Sunbeams to warm you,
Moonbeams to charm you,
Sheltering angels
so nothing can harm you.
Laughter to cheer you.
Wisdom to steer you.
And when you pray,
For Heaven to hear you.
Blessing